AUDIO ACCESS INCLUDED

MW00580951

JAZZ CHORD SOLOS
for TENOR UKULELE

10 Standards Arranged for Tenor Ukulele in Standard Notation and Tablature

To access audio visit:
www.halleonard.com/mylibrary

Enter Code
6770-9937-7617-7268

Arrangements by Howard Heitmeyer and Craig Brandau

as performed by Craig Brandau

ISBN 978-1-4584-3710-5

HAL•LEONARD®
CORPORATION
7777 W. BLUEMOUND RD. P.O. BOX 13819 MILWAUKEE, WI 53213

Visit Hal Leonard Online at
www.halleonard.com

PREFACE

This collection combines arrangements created both by Howard Heitmeyer and myself. "Here, There and Everywhere" is my own arrangement and all of the pieces are transcriptions of my recorded performances and do not necessarily reflect how they were originally written. This accounts for the various odd measures in some of the songs. Included with this book are audio tracks that will allow one to hear the songs in context and glean the proper timing and phrasing. Though several of the recorded tracks include a bass, these arrangements stand on their own and can be played as complete solos. Each piece provides its own set of challenges, but I find "Here, There and Everywhere" the easiest and "Mona Lisa" the most difficult of the group.

I hope you enjoy this compilation and that the arrangements will spark your own creativity.

—Craig Brandau

Howard Heitmeyer

Craig Brandau

CONTENTS

Here, There and Everywhere

Words and Music by John Lennon and Paul McCartney

Low G tuning:
(low to high) G-C-E-A

Intro
Freely

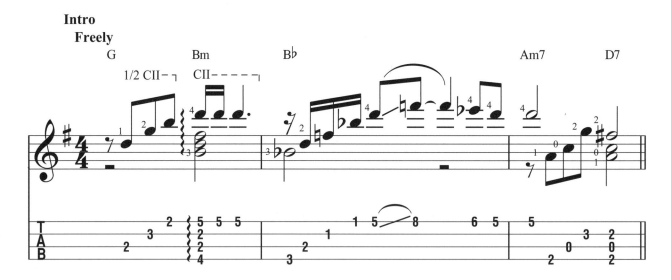

A **Moderately**

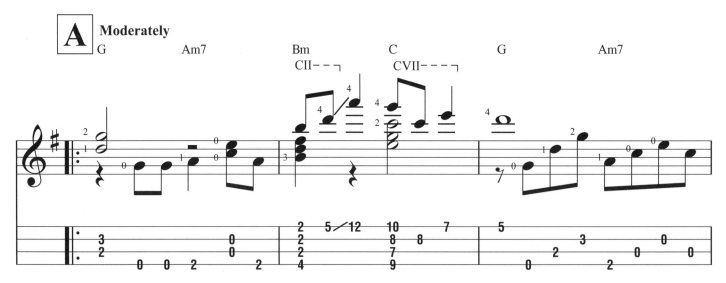

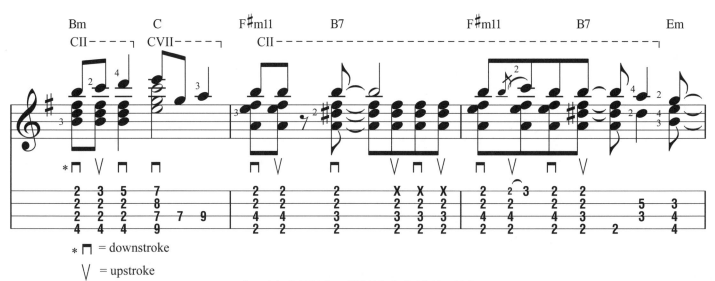

* ⊓ = downstroke

∨ = upstroke

*Harp Harmonic: The note is fretted normally and a harmonic is produced by
gently resting the right hand's index finger 12 frets (one octave) above
the indicated fret while the right hand's thumb assists by plucking the appropriate string.

Here's That Rainy Day
from CARNIVAL IN FLANDERS

TRACK 2

Words by Johnny Burke
Music by Jimmy Van Heusen

Low G tuning:
(low to high) G-C-E-A

Intro
Freely

A

Slow

Honeysuckle Rose
from AIN'T MISBEHAVIN'
Words by Andy Razaf
Music by Thomas "Fats" Waller

Low G tuning:
(low to high) G-C-E-A

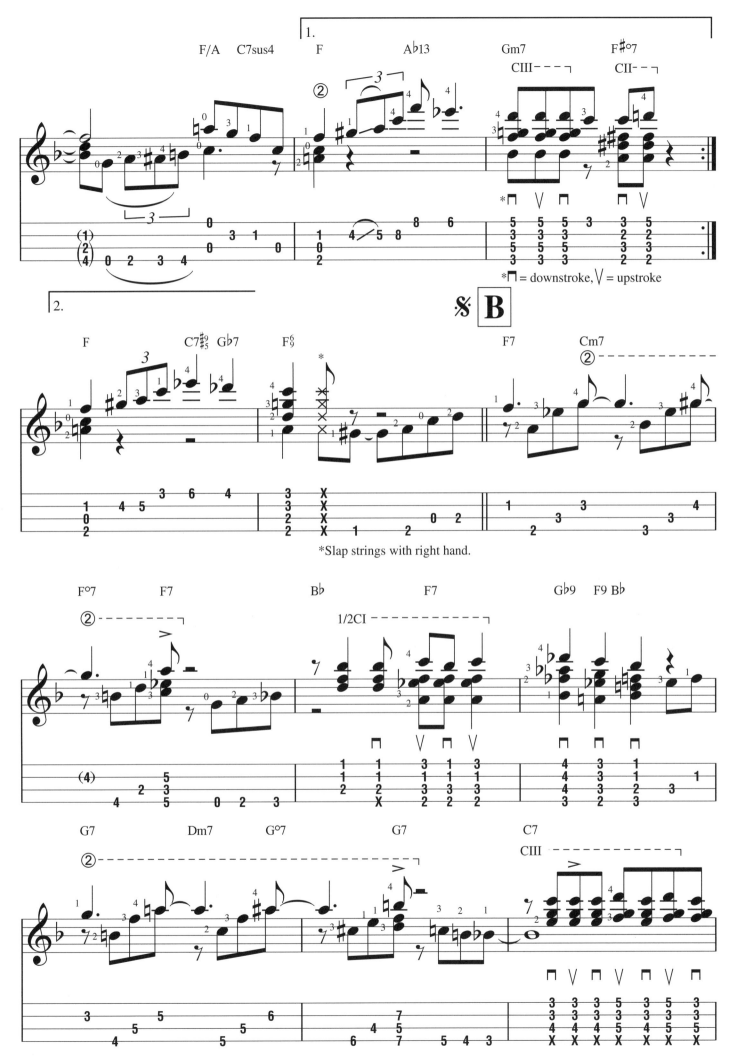

*□ = downstroke, ∨ = upstroke

*Slap strings with right hand.

*As before.

D.S. al Coda   Coda

Moon River

from the Paramount Picture BREAKFAST AT TIFFANY'S

TRACK 5

Words by Johnny Mercer
Music by Henry Mancini

Low G tuning:
(low to high) G-C-E-A

Intro
Slow waltz

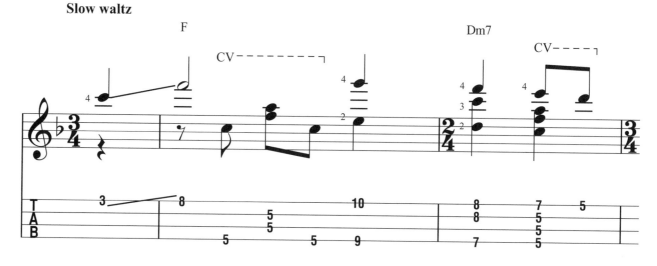

A

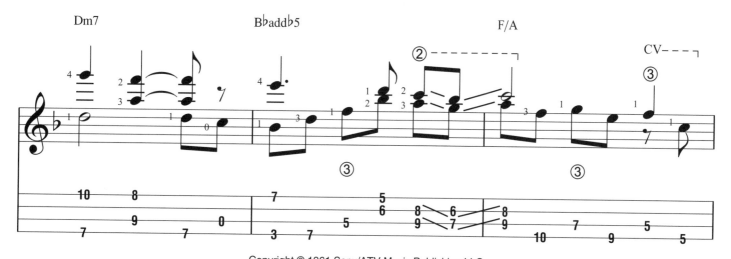

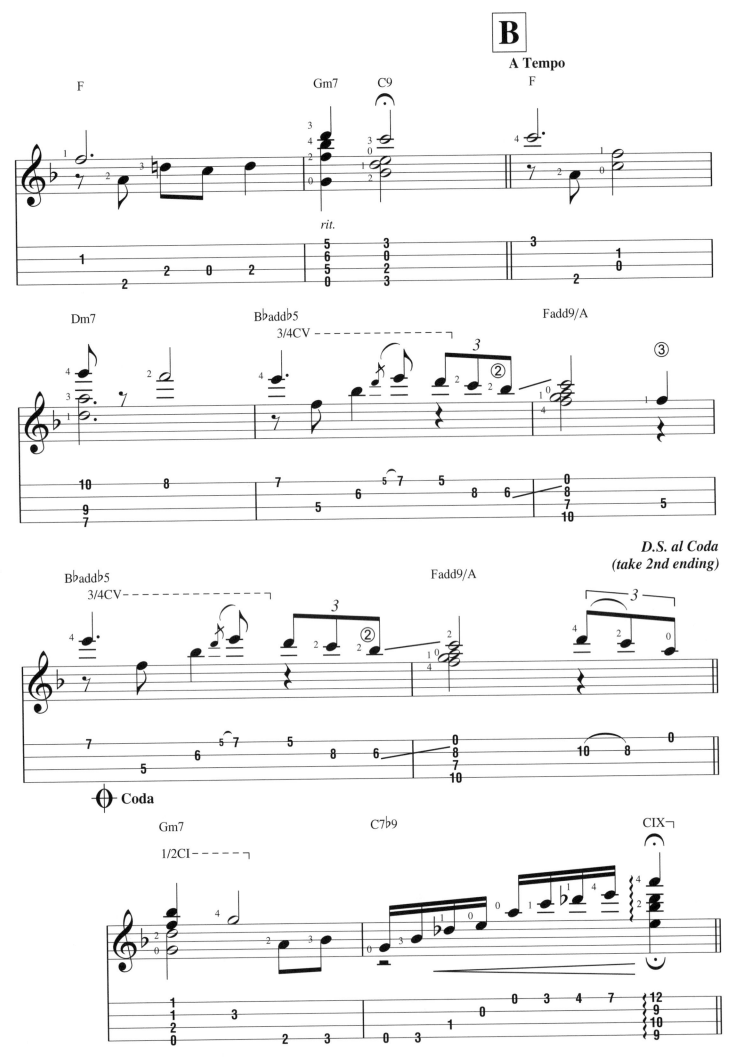

TRACK 4

Mona Lisa
from the Paramount Picture CAPTAIN CAREY, U.S.A.

Words and Music by Jay Livingston and Ray Evans

Low G tuning
(low to high) G-C-E-A

Intro
Freely

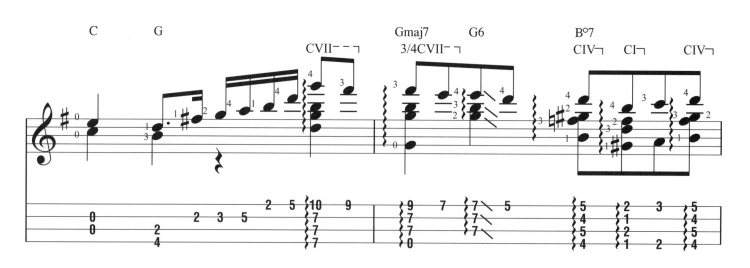

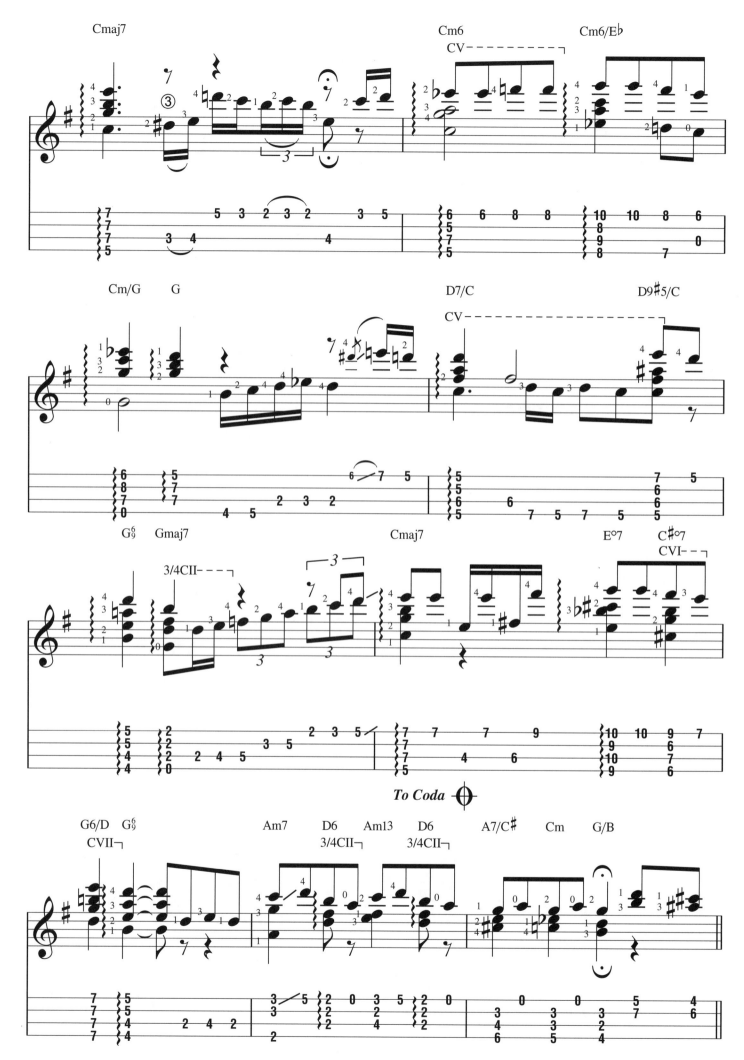

Tenderly
from TORCH SONG
Lyric by Jack Lawrence
Music by Walter Gross

Low G tuning:
(low to high) G-C-E-A

Intro
Freely

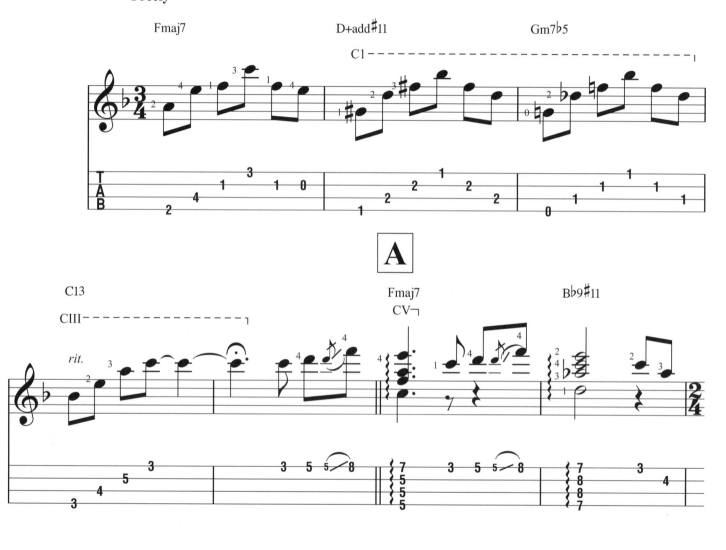

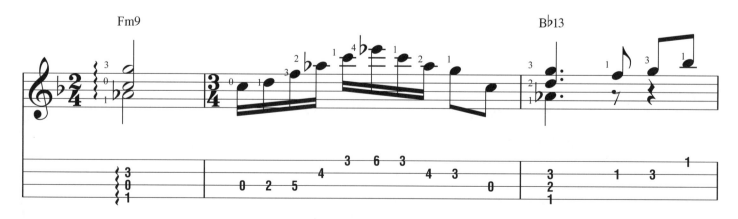

* ⊓ = downstroke

Till There Was You

from Meredith Willson's THE MUSIC MAN

By Meredith Willson

Low G tuning:
(low to high) G-C-E-A

Intro
Slow

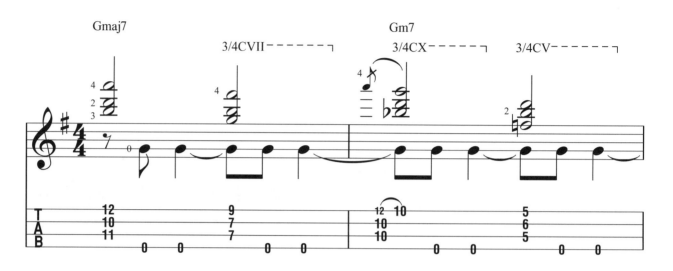

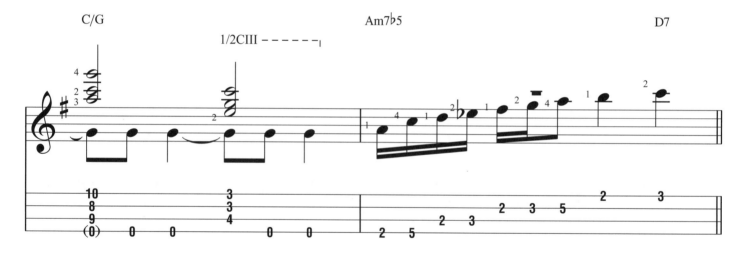

A

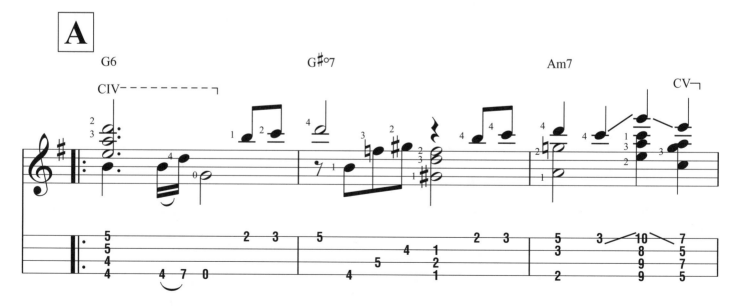

*Harp Harmonic: The note is fretted normally and a harmonic is produced by
gently resting the right hand's index finger 12 frets (one octave) above
the indicated fret while the right hand's thumb assists by plucking the appropriate string.

Wave

Words and Music by Antonio Carlos Jobim

TRACK 8

Low G tuning:
(low to high) G-C-E-A

Intro
Moderate Bossa Nova

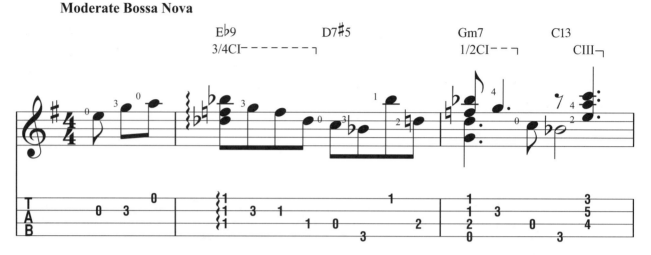

A

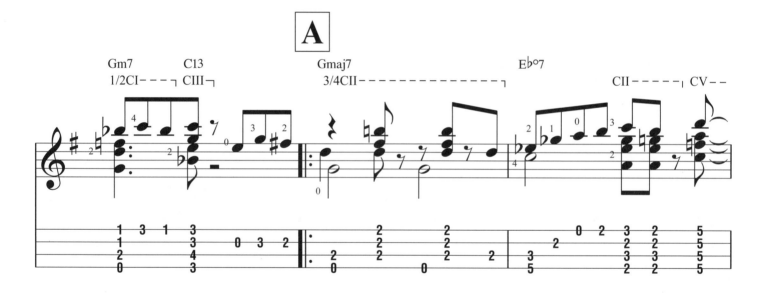

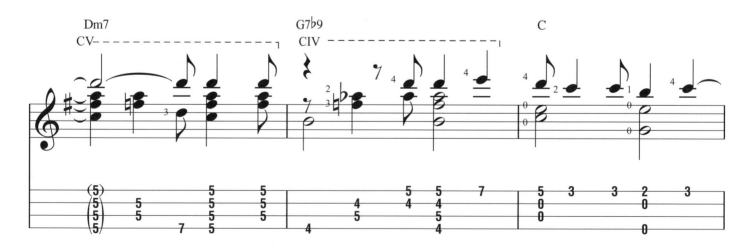

*⊓ = downstroke, ∨ = upstroke

When You Wish Upon a Star

from Walt Disney's PINOCCHIO

Words by Ned Washington
Music by Leigh Harline

Low G tuning:
(low to high) G-C-E-A

Intro
Slow

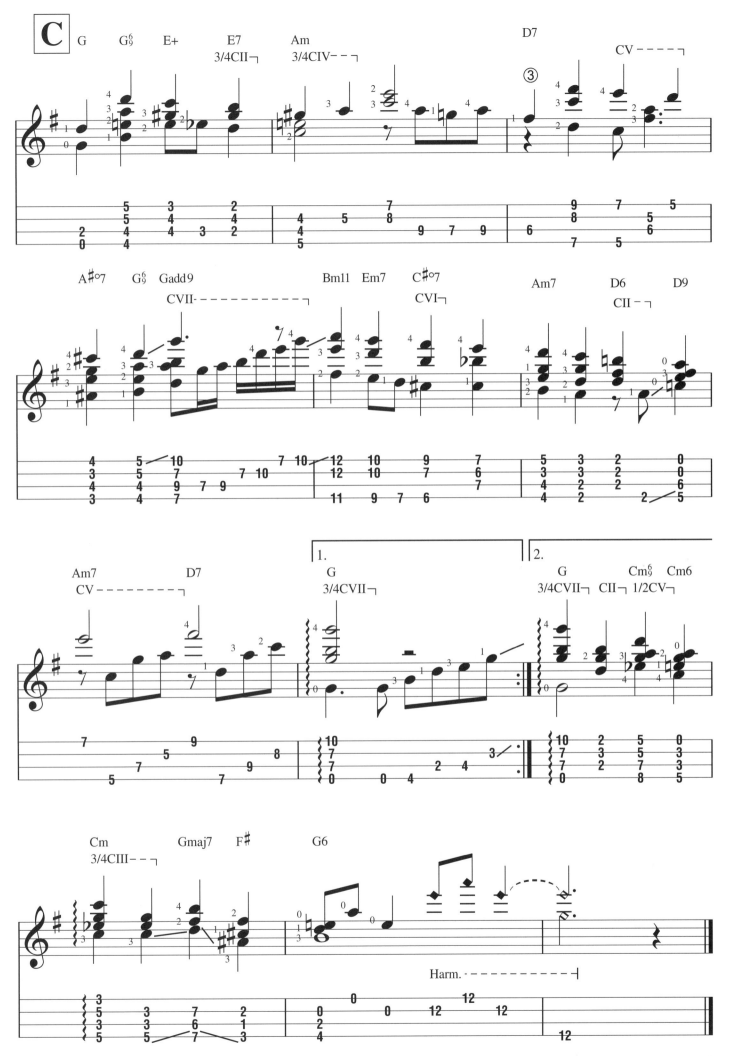

What a Wonderful World

Words and Music by George David Weiss and Bob Thiele

TRACK 9

Low G tuning:
(low to high) G-C-E-A

Intro
    Slow

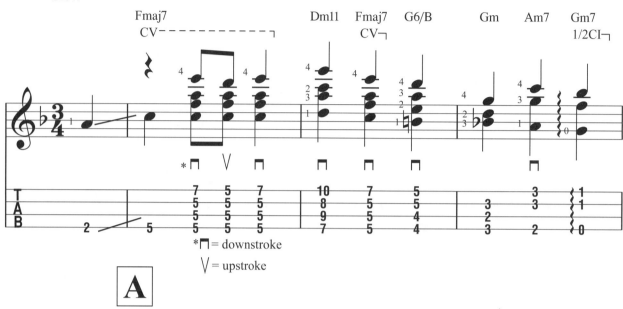

*◻ = downstroke

V = upstroke

A

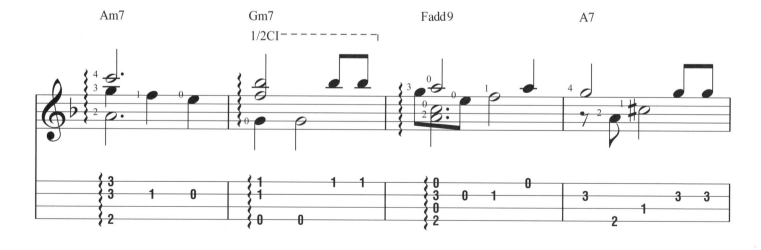

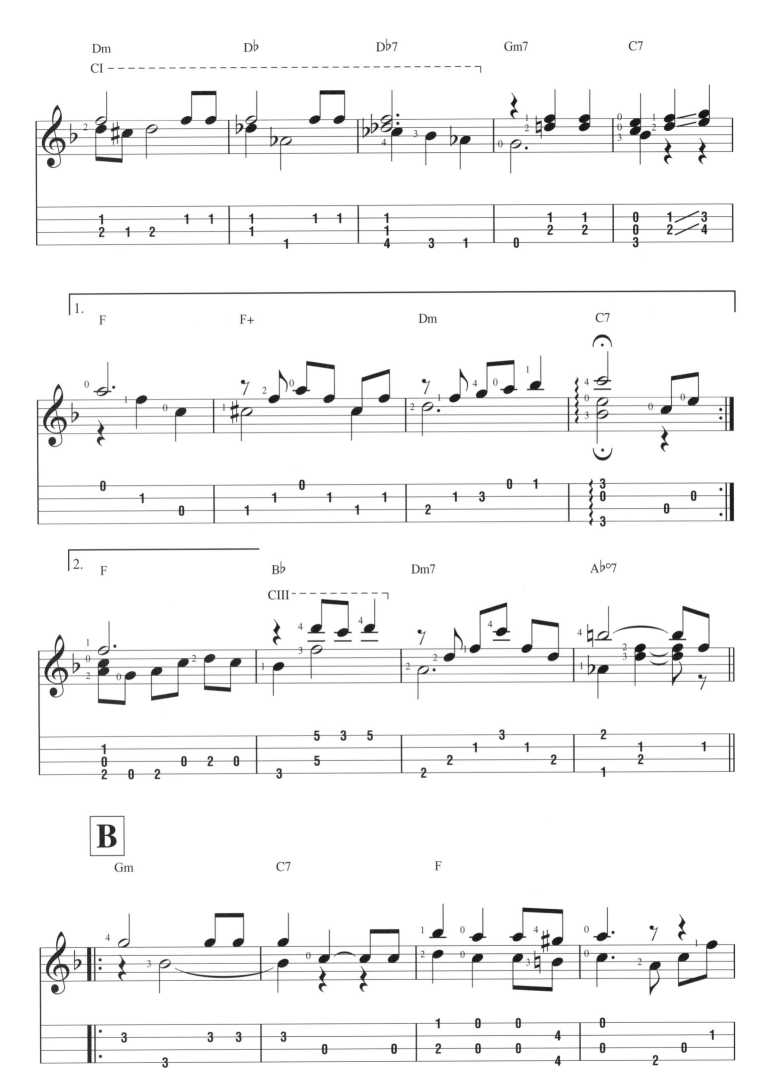

*Harp Harmonic: The note is fretted normally and a harmonic is produced by gently resting the right hand's index finger 12 frets (one octave) above the indicated fret while the right hand's thumb assists by plucking the appropriate string.

UKULELE NOTATION LEGEND

THE MUSICAL STAFF shows pitches and rhythms and is divided by bar lines into measures. Pitches are named after the first seven letters of the alphabet.

TABLATURE graphically represents the ukulele fingerboard. Each horizontal line represents a a string, and each number represents a fret.

2nd string, 3rd fret   1st & 2nd strings open, played together   open F chord

HALF-STEP BEND: Strike the note and bend up 1/2 step.

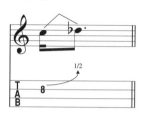

WHOLE-STEP BEND: Strike the note and bend up one step.

GRACE NOTE BEND: Strike the note and immediately bend up as indicated.

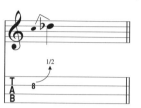

SLIGHT (MICROTONE) BEND: Strike the note and bend up 1/4 step.

BEND AND RELEASE: Strike the note and bend up as indicated, then release back to the original note. Only the first note is struck.

PRE-BEND: Bend the note as indicated, then strike it.

VIBRATO: The string is vibrated by rapidly bending and releasing the note with the fretting hand.

HAMMER-ON: Strike the first (lower) note with one finger, then sound the higher note (on the same string) with another finger by fretting it without picking.

PULL-OFF: Place both fingers on the notes to be sounded. Strike the first note and without picking, pull the finger off to sound the second (lower) note.

LEGATO SLIDE: Strike the first note and then slide the same fret-hand finger up or down to the second note. The second note is not struck.

SHIFT SLIDE: Same as legato slide, except the second note is struck.

TRILL: Very rapidly alternate between the notes indicated by continuously hammering on and pulling off.

TREMOLO PICKING: The note is picked as rapidly and continuously as possible.

NOTE: Tablature numbers in parentheses mean:

1. The note is being sustained over a system (note in standard notation is tied), or

2. The note is sustained, but a new articulation (such as a hammer-on, pull-off, slide or vibrato) begins, or

3. The note is a barely audible "ghost" note (note in standard notation is also in parentheses).

Additional Musical Definitions

(accent) • Accentuate note (play it louder)

(staccato) • Play the note short

D.S. al Coda • Go back to the sign (𝄋), then play until the measure marked "***To Coda***," then skip to the section labelled "**Coda**."

D.C. al Fine • Go back to the beginning of the song and play until the measure marked "***Fine***" (end).

N.C. • No chord.

 • Repeat measures between signs.

• When a repeated section has different endings, play the first ending only the first time and the second ending only the second time.

Ride the Ukulele Wave!

The Beach Boys for Ukulele

This folio features 20 favorites, including: Barbara Ann • Be True to Your School • California Girls • Fun, Fun, Fun • God Only Knows • Good Vibrations • Help Me Rhonda • I Get Around • In My Room • Kokomo • Little Deuce Coupe • Sloop John B • Surfin' U.S.A. • Wouldn't It Be Nice • and more!
00701726 . . . . $14.99

Disney Songs for Ukulele

20 great Disney classics arranged for all uke players, including: Beauty and the Beast • Bibbidi-Bobbidi-Boo (The Magic Song) • Can You Feel the Love Tonight • Chim Chim Cher-ee • Heigh-Ho • It's a Small World • Some Day My Prince Will Come • We're All in This Together • When You Wish upon a Star • and more.
00701708 . . . . $12.99

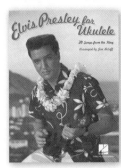

Elvis Presley for Ukulele

arr. Jim Beloff

20 classic hits from The King: All Shook Up • Blue Hawaii • Blue Suede Shoes • Can't Help Falling in Love • Don't • Heartbreak Hotel • Hound Dog • Jailhouse Rock • Love Me • Love Me Tender • Return to Sender • Suspicious Minds • Teddy Bear • and more.
00701004 . . . . $14.99

The Beatles for Ukulele

Ukulele players can strum, sing and pick along with 20 Beatles classics! Includes: All You Need Is Love • Eight Days a Week • Good Day Sunshine • Here, There and Everywhere • Let It Be • Love Me Do • Penny Lane • Yesterday • and more.
00700154 . . . . $16.99

Folk Songs for Ukulele

A great collection to take along to the campfire! 60 folk songs, including: Amazing Grace • Buffalo Gals • Camptown Races • For He's a Jolly Good Fellow • Good Night Ladies • Home on the Range • I've Been Working on the Railroad • Kumbaya • My Bonnie Lies over the Ocean • On Top of Old Smoky • Scarborough Fair • Swing Low, Sweet Chariot • Take Me Out to the Ball Game • Yankee Doodle • and more.
00696068 . . . . $12.99

Hawaiian Songs for Ukulele

Over thirty songs from the state that made the ukulele famous, including: Beyond the Rainbow • Hanalei Moon • Ka-lu-a • Lovely Hula Girl • Mele Kalikimaka • One More Aloha • Sea Breeze • Tiny Bubbles • Waikiki • and more.
00696065 . . . . $9.99

Irving Berlin Songs Arranged for the "Uke"

20 great songs with full instructions, including: Always • Blue Skies • Easter Parade • How Deep Is the Ocean (How High Is the Sky) • A Pretty Girl Is like a Melody • Say It with Music • What'll I Do? • White Christmas • and more.
00005558 . . . . $6.95

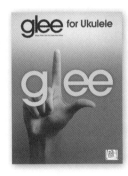

Glee

Music from the Fox Television Show for Ukulele

20 favorites for Gleeks to strum and sing, including: Bad Romance • Beautiful • Defying Gravity • Don't Stop Believin' • No Air • Proud Mary • Rehab • True Colors • and more.
00701722 . . . $14.99

Worship Songs for Ukulele

25 worship songs: Amazing Grace (My Chains are Gone) • Blessed Be Your Name • Enough • God of Wonders • Holy Is the Lord • How Great Is Our God • In Christ Alone • Love the Lord • Mighty to Save • Sing to the King • Step by Step • We Fall Down • and more.
00702546 . . . . $12.99

The Daily Ukulele

compiled and arranged by Liz and Jim Beloff

Strum a different song everyday with easy arrangements of 365 of your favorite songs in one big songbook! Includes favorites by the Beatles, Beach Boys, and Bob Dylan, folk songs, pop songs, kids' songs, Christmas carols, and Broadway and Hollywood tunes, all with a spiral binding for ease of use.
00240356 . . . . $34.99

Jake Shimabukuro – Peace Love Ukulele

Deemed "the Hendrix of the ukulele," Hawaii native Jake Shimabukuro is a uke virtuoso. Our songbook features note-for-note transcriptions with ukulele tablature of Jake's masterful playing on all the CD tracks: Bohemian Rhapsody • Boy Meets Girl • Bring Your Adz • Hallelujah • Pianoforte 2010 • Variation on a Dance 2010 • and more, plus two bonus selections!
00702516 . . . . $19.99

Rodgers & Hammerstein for Ukulele

arr. Jim Beloff

Now you can play 20 classic show tunes from this beloved songwriting duo on your uke! Includes: All at Once You Love Her • Do-Re-Mi • Edelweiss • Getting to Know You • Impossible • My Favorite Things • and more.
00701905 . . . . $12.99

HAL•LEONARD® CORPORATION

7777 W. Bluemound Rd. P.O. Box 13819 Milwaukee, WI 53213

0212

HAL•LEONARD UKULELE PLAY-ALONG

Now you can play your favorite songs on your uke with great-sounding backing tracks to help you sound like a bona fide pro!

1. POP HITS
American Pie • Copacabana (At the Copa) • Crocodile Rock • Kokomo • Lean on Me • Stand by Me • Twist and Shout • What the World Needs Now Is Love.
00701451 Book/CD Pack $14.99

2. UKE CLASSICS
Ain't She Sweet • Five Foot Two, Eyes of Blue (Has Anybody Seen My Girl?) • It's Only a Paper Moon • Living in the Sunlight, Loving in the Moonlight • Pennies from Heaven • Tonight You Belong to Me • Ukulele Lady • When I'm Cleaning Windows.
00701452 Book/CD Pack $12.99

3. HAWAIIAN FAVORITES
Aloha Oe • Blue Hawaii • HarborLights • The Hawaiian Wedding Song (Ke Kali Nei Au) • Mele Kalikimaka • Sleepy Lagoon • Sweet Someone • Tiny Bubbles.
00701453 Book/CD Pack $12.99

4. CHILDREN'S SONGS
Do-Re-Mi • The Hokey Pokey • It's a Small World • My Favorite Things • Puff the Magic Dragon • Sesame Street Theme • Splish Splash • This Land Is Your Land.
00701454 Book/CD Pack $12.99

5. CHRISTMAS SONGS
Do You Hear What I Hear • Feliz Navidad • Frosty the Snow Man • Here Comes Santa Claus (Right down Santa Claus Lane) • Jingle-Bell Rock • Nuttin' for Christmas • Rudolph the Red-Nosed Reindeer • Santa Claus Is Comin' to Town.
00701696 Book/CD Pack $12.99

6. LENNON & McCARTNEY
And I Love Her • Day Tripper • Here, There and Everywhere • Hey Jude • Let It Be • Norwegian Wood (This Bird Has Flown) • Nowhere Man • Yesterday.
00701723 Book/CD Pack $12.99

7. DISNEY FAVORITES
Alice in Wonderland • The Bare Necessities • Candle on the Water • Chim Chim Cher-ee • A Dream Is a Wish Your Heart Makes • Mickey Mouse March • Supercalifragilisticexpialidocious • Under the Sea.
00701724 Book/CD Pack $12.99

8. CHART HITS
All the Right Moves • Bubbly • Hey, Soul Sister • I'm Yours • Toes • Use Somebody • Viva la Vida • You're Beautiful.
00701745 Book/CD Pack $14.99

9. THE SOUND OF MUSIC
Climb Ev'ry Mountain • Do-Re-Mi • Edelweiss • Maria • My Favorite Things • Sixteen Going on Seventeen • Something Good • The Sound of Music.
00701784 Book/CD Pack $12.99

10. MOTOWN
Baby Love • Easy • How Sweet It Is (To Be Loved by You) • I Heard It Through the Grapevine • I Want You Back • My Cherie Amour • My Girl • You Can't Hurry Love.
00701964 Book/CD Pack $12.99

11. CHRISTMAS STRUMMING
Away in a Manger • Deck the Hall • The First Noel • Hark! the Herald Angels Sing • Jingle Bells • Joy to the World • O Come, All Ye Faithful (Adeste Fideles) • We Three Kings of Orient Are.
00702458 Book/CD Pack $12.99

12. BLUEGRASS FAVORITES
Angel Band • Dooley • Fox on the Run • I Am a Man of Constant Sorrow • I'll Fly Away • Keep on the Sunny Side • Sitting on Top of the World • With Body and Soul.
00702584 Book/CD Pack $12.99

13. UKULELE SONGS
Daughter • Dream a Little Dream of Me • Elderly Woman Behind the Counter in a Small Town • Last Kiss • More Than You Know • Sleepless Nights • Tonight You Belong to Me • Yellow Ledbetter.
00702599 Book/CD Pack $12.99

14. JOHNNY CASH
Cry, Cry, Cry • Daddy Sang Bass • Folsom Prison Blues • Hey, Porter • I Walk the Line • Jackson • (Ghost) Riders in the Sky (A Cowboy Legend) • Ring of Fire.
00702615 Book/CD Pack $14.99

15. COUNTRY CLASSICS
Achy Breaky Heart (Don't Tell My Heart) • Chattahoochee • Crazy • King of the Road • Rocky Top • Tennessee Waltz • You Are My Sunshine • Your Cheatin' Heart.
00702834 Book/CD Pack $12.99

16. STANDARDS
Ain't Misbehavin' • All of Me • Beyond the Sea • Georgia on My Mind • Mister Sandman • Moon River • That's Amoré (That's Love) • Unchained Melody.
00702835 Book/CD Pack $12.99

17. POP STANDARDS
Every Breath You Take • Fields of Gold • I Just Called to Say I Love You • Kansas City • Killing Me Softly with His Song • Sunny • Tears in Heaven • What a Wonderful World.
00702836 Book/CD Pack $12.99

23. TAYLOR SWIFT
Crazier • Fearless • Love Story • Mean • Our Song • Teardrops on My Guitar • White Horse • You Belong with Me.
00704106 Book/CD Pack $14.99

24. WINTER WONDERLAND
All I Want for Christmas Is My Two Front Teeth • Blue Christmas • The Christmas Song (Chestnuts Roasting on an Open Fire) • Have Yourself a Merry Little Christmas • Let It Snow! Let It Snow! Let It Snow! • Little Saint Nick • Sleigh Ride • Winter Wonderland.
00101871 Book/CD Pack $12.99

HAL•LEONARD® CORPORATION

7777 W. BLUEMOUND RD. P.O. BOX 13819 MILWAUKEE, WI 53213

www.halleonard.com

Prices, contents, and availability subject to change without notice.

0912